RETREAT
GUIDE

A WOMAN CLOTHED
WITH THE SUN

AN ADVENT RETREAT GUIDE
ON OUR LADY OF GUADALUPE

FR. JOHN BARTUNEK, LC, STHD

This booklet is a part of RCSpirituality's *Retreat Guide* service, which includes free online videos and audio tracks available at **RCSpirituality.org**.

INTRODUCTION

A Woman Clothed with the Sun

RETREAT OVERVIEW

During Advent in the year 1531 the Blessed Virgin Mary appeared to a native Mexican, St. Juan Diego, and asked him a favor. She sent him to the bishop with a request to have a Catholic church built on the hill where she was appearing—Tepeyac Hill—in present-day Mexico City. The bishop was skeptical. He responded to the petition with a request of his own. He asked for a sign to show that this request truly was coming from God. When Juan Diego relayed this to Mary, she complied—she provided a wonderful, dramatic sign indeed.

She left her image emblazoned on Juan Diego's tunic, called a tilma. This miraculous image—still in existence five centuries later, known throughout the world as Our Lady of Guadalupe, and still inexplicable even to modern science—convinced the skeptical bishop and made an incalculable impact on the evangelization of the Americas, an impact that continues to resound and spread even today.

These events, and that impact, are the subject of this Advent Retreat Guide: A Woman Clothed with the Sun.

o   The First Meditation will unpack the events as they unfolded, showing how they echo the meaning of Advent.

o   The Second Meditation will explore the actual words of Our Lady in her conversation with St. Juan Diego, words that beautifully echo the meaning of Christmas.

o   The Conference will reflect on the symbolism present in the image itself, symbolism that can help stir up the spirit of Christmas in our souls.

Let's begin by quieting our hearts and turning our attention to the Lord, who never stops paying attention to us. Let's ask him for all the graces we need, and let's open our hearts to whatever graces he wants to send us through our contemplation of Our Lady of Guadalupe, a woman clothed with the sun.

NOTES

FIRST MEDITATION

A New-World Christmas

guʒmā.   mc

INTRODUCTION

At the time of Our Lady of Guadalupe's apparitions in 1531, Christians had only recently arrived in America. Christopher Columbus landed in San Salvador back in 1492, but Europeans didn't make it to Mexico until 1517. And the first missionaries didn't arrive there until 1522, a year after the Spanish conquistador Hernán Cortes had toppled the Aztec Empire and conquered their capital, now known as Mexico City. An official Spanish governing authority wasn't set up until 1528. Soon afterwards, trouble began brewing between government officials and missionaries, who had conflicting ideas about how to interact with the native Mexicans. This conflict even led to an assassination attempt against the bishop-elect, the same Franciscan Friar who would receive the sign from Our Lady and oversee the building of the first chapel on Tepeyac hill.

TROUBLED AND UNCERTAIN TIMES

We can imagine how unstable and tense the situation must have been. The Aztec Empire itself had been riddled with tribal conflict and political instability. The Spaniards had exploited and exacerbated that in their own efforts of conquest, and now were facing division among themselves. Just on a political level, then, high-strung tensions ran in three different directions: between the Spaniards and the native Mexicans; between the cultures of the different groups of native Mexicans; and between the Spanish missionaries and the Spanish overlords.

But the problems didn't end there. As part of their Aztec conquest, the Spaniards forcibly squelched the native Mexican religious practices, which were extremely elaborate and included human sacrifice. The abrupt cessation of traditional religion on top of the political conquest must have created profound and widespread disorientation and concern among the Mexicans. When the year 1531 began and unfolded with a series of notable natural phenomena—including earthquakes, a solar eclipse, and a sighting of Halley's Comet—it is understandable how this led to an undercurrent of incipient panic and rumors about the end of the world.

A LIGHT IN THE DARKNESS

Into this swirling historical, cultural and political turbulence stepped Our Lady of Guadalupe. It happened in 1531 between December 9th and December 12th, during the winter solstice, a period of significance for the traditional Mexican religions.

During those days, Juan Diego, a native Mexican commoner who had been baptized five years earlier, was making his way to Mexico City for prayer and instruction when he heard beautiful, otherworldly music from the top of Tepeyac hill. When the music stopped, a woman's voice called out to him, and he went up to the top of the hill, where he beheld a beautiful woman adorned in clothing that shone like the sun.

This was Our Lady's first apparition, on December 9th (now St. Juan Diego's feast day), in which she instructed Juan Diego to ask the bishop to build a church on that hill, formerly a place of pagan worship. Juan Diego's first attempt failed, but when he went back to the hill, reported, and advised Our Lady to choose a more illustrious messenger than himself, she only reiterated her desire and told him to return to the bishop on the following day and repeat her request. He did so, and in that second meeting, after questioning him in great detail, the bishop asked for a sign.

FACING OBSTACLES

When Juan Diego reported this to the Blessed Virgin, she promised to provide a sign for the bishop on the following day. But the following day, December 11th, Juan Diego wasn't able to come back. He had to find a doctor for his uncle, who had fallen violently ill and seemed to be on the point of death.

Even the doctor couldn't help, however. So on December 12th (currently the feast day of Our Lady of Guadalupe) his uncle asked Juan Diego to bring him a priest to help prepare him to die. So the future saint headed back along the nine-mile trek to Mexico City.

When he passed by Tepeyac hill, he took a roundabout path, trying to dodge the beautiful lady, since he had urgent family affairs to tend to. But in this her fourth appearance, Mary actually descended from the hill in order to meet him on his way. In their conversation, she told him she herself would take care of his uncle, while he should go back to the top of the hill and gather the flowers there, then bring them back to her so she could arrange them. Then he was to take them to the bishop, and that would be his sign, since such a variety of flowers didn't grow in that place, and since flowers didn't grow there at that time of year in any case. He obeyed her indications, and Mary arranged the flowers, which Juan Diego had cut and then held in his tilma.

AN EARLY CHRISTMAS PRESENT

Upon his return to the bishop's residence, Juan Diego was forced to wait outside—opposition and lies about his intentions had already surrounded him with suspicion. But eventually the curious servants forced a glimpse of the flowers—which Juan Diego was supposed to show only to the bishop—and then brought him inside. Juan Diego knelt in front of the bishop and reported the Virgin's message, then unfolded his tilma, spilling the flowers onto the floor and revealing, to the amazement of everyone, the image of the Blessed Virgin emblazoned on the course fabric of his tilma.

Everyone present—the servants as well as the bishop himself and assistant— fell to their knees, overwhelmed. The bishop tearfully begged forgiveness for his earlier skepticism, invited Juan Diego to stay in his residence, and reverently brought the tilma into his own private chapel. The very next day, they went together to Tepeyac hill and began the construction of a chapel on the site of the apparitions. The small building was finished by Christmas, and the miraculous image of the Virgin was put on display there after a sacred procession from the bishop's house on December 26th.

ECHOES OF ADVENT

Other wonders accompanied this dramatic series of encounters—like the miraculous healing of Juan Diego's uncle and Our Lady's appearance to him as well (in fact, she told the uncle that the image should be called "Our Lady of Guadalupe"). But even this simple narration of the basic events shows just how much the story of Our Lady of Guadalupe is an Advent story.

Our fallen world, into which Jesus was born at Christmas, was and is no different than Mexico in 1531, filled as it always has been with religious, cultural, and political conflicts, with fear, suffering, and uncertainty. Every year at Christmas, we celebrate the immense love of God that moved Jesus not to abandon us in our misery, but to move right in with us, just as he wanted to do again by having the bishop build a church on Tepeyac hill.

The Virgin Mary, when God chose her to be the mother of our Lord, was a humble and obscure young woman. From the world's perspective, Juan Diego too was an unlikely candidate to become involved in marvelous, miraculous, history-altering events.

ANOTHER KIND OF INCARNATION

Mary's choice of a sign, emblazoning her colorful, ornate image on the coarse fabric of a common tilma, also fits with the mystery of Christmas. In Mexican culture at the time, plain tilmas indicated common social status, and colorful, decorated tilmas indicated aristocratic status. Symbolically, then, the image of Our Lady of Guadalupe elevated Juan Diego's social standing, just as Jesus taking human nature upon himself elevates all of us who believe in him to become, as St. John's Gospel puts it, "children of God" (John 1:12). And even more remarkably, Mary's features and clothing on the tilma image depict her as a native Mexican herself: to help them discover the true God and his infinite love, she, in a sense, became one of them, just as Jesus had done through his incarnation all those centuries before: "And the word became flesh, and made his dwelling among us" (John 1:14).

In the next Meditation, we will examine some of the words that Mary spoke to Juan Diego. But for now, let's take some time, in the quiet of our hearts, to prayerfully reflect on the Advent message contained in these awe-inspiring events from 1531. The following questions and quotations may help your meditation.

QUESTIONS FOR PERSONAL REFLECTION/GROUP DISCUSSION

1. How firmly do I believe that God is interested in the struggles I am facing, just as he was interested in the struggles being faced by his people in Mexico in 1531?

2. How deeply am I convinced that God chooses every Christian (including myself), no matter how humble or limited, to be his messenger in this world and to help spread his Kingdom, just as the Virgin Mary chose Juan Diego?

3. The image of Our Lady of Guadalupe depicts Mary with features and clothing familiar to and approachable by the native Mexican people. How personal and relevant to my day-to-day life is my own Marian devotion? What can I do to make it more personal and relevant?

QUOTATIONS TO HELP YOUR PRAYER

He was in the world, and the world came to be through him, but the world did not know him. He came to what was his own, but his own people did not accept him. But to those who did accept him he gave power to become children of God, to those who believe in his name, who were born not by natural generation nor by human choice nor by a man's decision but of God. And the Word became flesh and made his dwelling among us, and we saw his glory, the glory as of the Father's only Son, full of grace and truth.

—John 1:10–14
NABRE

At the birth of Jesus, the Magi came from the East to Bethlehem and "saw the child with Mary his Mother" (Mt 2:11). At the beginning of his public life, at the marriage of Cana, when the Son of God works the first of his signs, awakening faith in the disciples, it is Mary who intervenes and directs the servants towards her Son in these words: "Do whatever he tells you" (Jn 2:5). In this regard I once wrote that "the Mother of Christ presents herself as the spokeswoman of her Son's will, pointing out those things which must be done so that the salvific power of the Messiah may be manifested". For this reason Mary is the sure path to our meeting with Christ. Devotion to the Mother of the Lord, when it is genuine, is always an impetus to a life guided by the spirit and values of the Gospel.

—*Ecclesia in America*, 11
ST. JOHN PAUL II

My son, perform your tasks in meekness;
    then you will be loved by those
    whom God accepts.
The greater you are, the more you must
humble yourself;

so you will find favor in the sight of the Lord.
For great is the might of the Lord;
    he is glorified by the humble.
Seek not what is too difficult for you,
    nor investigate what is beyond your power.
Reflect upon what has been assigned to you,
    for you do not need what is hidden.

—Sirach 3:17–20
NABRE

NOTES

SECOND MEDITATION

Words of Comfort and Joy

INTRODUCTION

News of Mary's apparitions spread rapidly. Natives and Spaniards alike began to visit the chapel on Tepeyac in droves, listening to Juan Diego's story and gazing at the miraculous image. And so, even before the political situation started to improve, huge numbers of native Mexicans began to entrust themselves to the Virgin Mary's care and receive instruction in the Christian faith, something they had been reluctant to do after the destruction of their Aztec temple worship. One contemporary historian put it like this:

> [The Indians], submerged in profound darkness, still loved and served false little gods, clay figurines and images of our enemy the devil, in spite of having heard about the faith. But when they heard that the Holy Mother of Our Lord Jesus Christ had appeared, and since they saw and admired her most perfect Image, which has no human art, their eyes were opened as if suddenly day had dawned for them.[1]

In subsequent centuries, skeptics have questioned the authenticity of the apparitions and the image, but the overwhelming witness of history shows that the native peoples themselves were so convinced of the divine origin of Our Lady of Guadalupe that the previous trickle of converts to Christianity became a flood of tens of thousands in just a few years. Even today, Mexico City's shrine of Our Lady of Guadalupe is the most visited Marian shrine in the world, annually attracting an estimated 20 million pilgrims.

---

[1]   All the quotations included in this Meditation are taken from *Our Lady of Guadalupe: Mother of the Civilization of Love*, by Carl Anderson and Msgr. Eduardo Chávez (Doubleday, New York: 2009).

A CHRISTMAS-LIKE MESSAGE

What is it about Our Lady of Guadalupe that has spoken so eloquently and powerfully to so many people over the course of so much time? Maybe part of the explanation lies in how deeply the message of Guadalupe shares in the unquenchable joyfulness, hopefulness, and charm of the Christmas message itself. Let's look, for example, at some of Our Lady's conversation with Juan Diego throughout the four apparitions.

When she first called Juan Diego up to the top of Tepeyac hill, where she appeared to him shining like the sun, and the light coming like waves from her clothes transformed even the landscape around her such that Juan Diego wondered if he had died and gone to heaven, she spoke to him in his native language, like this:

❝ Know, know for sure, my dearest and youngest son, that I am the ever-perfect holy Mary, who has the honor to be the mother of the true God by whom we all live, the Creator of people, the Lord of the near and far, the Lord of heaven and earth.

She invokes her motherly presence, the same presence that gives us all such comfort and warm inspiration throughout the season of Advent, and she introduces the Lord using divine titles that Juan Diego would have been familiar with. Some of the sages from his own Toltec culture had maintained an awareness of the existence of one superior God, above and beyond the other pagan gods worshiped in the Aztec pantheon. This divinity was viewed as Creator and Lord, but he dwelt far beyond the human realm and was considered absolutely inaccessible. The Virgin Mary, in this first apparition, taps into that vague intuition of religious truth, clarifying its meaning and revealing its limitations. She went on to say:

❡ I want very much that they build my sacred little house here, in which I will show Him, I will exalt Him upon making Him manifest, I will give Him to all people in all my personal love, Him that is my compassionate gaze, Him that is my help, Him that is my salvation. Because truly I am your compassionate Mother, yours and that of all the people that live together in this land, and also of all the other various lineages of men, those who love me, those who cry to me, those who seek me, those who trust in me. Because there [at my sacred house] truly will I hear their cry, their sadness, in order to remedy, to cure all their various troubles, their miseries, their pains.

Mary's desire to build her "sacred little house" there on Tepeyac hill, where she will manifest and give Christ to all the people, is a sixteenth-century extension of God's own desire to dwell among us, reveal himself to us, and grant us his saving grace—the desire that he fulfilled so wonderfully on the first Christmas.

A GENTLE OMNIPOTENCE

In these first words of Our Lady to Juan Diego, Mary communicates both God's power—she refers to him as the Creator of people and the Lord of heaven and earth—and also his gentleness, mercy and desire to be close to us.: Sshe calls Jesus: "Him that is my compassionate gaze, Him that is my help, Him that is my salvation" and she declares that through him her spiritual motherhood extends to "all the people of this land, and also all the other various lineages of men ..."

This is the great revelation of Christ: that the one true God, unlimited in power and glory, wishes to come and walk among us and be our companion. Announcing this inconceivable truth to the native Mexicans through a Marian apparition echoes God's own method of bringing Jesus into the world in the first place—through the cooperation of a humble, gentle maiden in a little stable cave in Bethlehem. Jesus will dwell in the "little house" that Our Lady of Guadalupe wants to be built, but Mary will be there too, her motherly presence reminding us all of God's tenderness and approachableness, which are such essential elements of the Christian message, and the Christmas season.

LIGHT IN THE DARKNESS

Later, when Juan Diego has already begun to suffer contradiction and opposition in his efforts to bring Mary's message to the bishop, and when anxiety for his uncle's life is disturbing his mind and saddening his heart, Mary again appears to him, comforting him with these words:

Listen, put it into your heart, my youngest son, that what frightened you, what afflicted you, is nothing; do not let it disturb your face, your heart; do not fear this sickness nor any other sickness, nor any sharp and hurtful thing. Am I not here, I who have the honor to be your Mother? Are you not in my shadow and under my protection? Am I not the source of your joy? Are you not in the hollow of my mantle, in the crossing of my arms? Do you need something more? Let nothing else worry you, disturb you …

Here we have Mary echoing another central message of Christmas, that although we often have to endure periods of darkness and suffering as we make our pilgrimage through this fallen world, we are not alone. God's unlimited goodness and power—in Christ and through his Church—are on our side. St. John puts it like this at the very beginning of his Gospel: "… the light shines in the darkness, and the darkness has not overcome it" (John 1:5).

In fact, the tone of Mary's words to Juan Diego strikingly resembles the tone of the message the angel gave to the shepherds on the first Christmas night:

> Do not be afraid; for behold, I proclaim to you good news of great joy that will be for all the people. For today in the city of David a savior has been born for you who is Messiah and Lord … Glory to God in the highest and on earth peace to those on whom his favor rests.
>
> —Luke 2:11–12, 14

This message, the invitation to hope and have confidence in God's grace, in Mary's intercession, even in the midst of contradiction and suffering, was reiterated cosmologically in the apparitions. The day on which Mary gave her sign to the bishop was the winter solstice of 1531, the shortest and darkest day of the year, after which the days would begin to get longer and the winter darkness would begin to recede.

GETTING BACK TO BASICS

Thinking about the words that Our Lady of Guadalupe spoke to Juan Diego can spark a fruitful reflection on the most basic truths of our Christian faith. And reflecting afresh on those truths, giving them time and space to seep more deeply into our minds and hearts, is what Advent, this season of preparation to celebrate Christmas, is all about.

In the Conference, we will move from reflecting on Our Lady of Guadalupe's words to reflecting on the meaning of the miraculous image itself. But for now, let's take some time, in the quiet of our hearts, to savor and celebrate those words. The following questions and quotations may help your meditation.

QUESTIONS FOR PERSONAL REFLECTION/GROUP DISCUSSION

1. What struck me the most from the words that she spoke to St. Juan Diego and why?

2. God chose to bring Jesus into the world through Mary, giving him a real, human mother, and giving all his followers in Mary a spiritual mother. In my own words, why do I think God made that choice?

3. How would I describe my personal devotion to the Blessed Virgin Mary? What could help bring it to the next level?

QUOTATIONS TO HELP YOUR PRAYER

I want very much that they build my sacred little house here, in which I will show Him, I will exalt Him upon making Him manifest, I will give Him to all people in all my personal love, Him that is my compassionate gaze, Him that is my help, Him that is my salvation. Because truly I am your compassionate Mother, yours and that of all the people that live together in this land, and also of all the other various lineages of men, those who love me, those who cry to me, those who seek me, those who trust in me. Because there [at my sacred house] truly will hear their cry, their sadness, in order to remedy, to cure all their various troubles, their miseries, their pains.

—The Nican Mopohua, 26–32

Listen, put it into your heart, my youngest son, that what frightened you, what afflicted you, is nothing; do not let it disturb your face, your heart; do not fear this sickness nor any other sickness, nor any sharp and hurtful thing. Am I not here, I who have the honor to be your Mother? Are you not in my shadow and under my protection? Am I not the source of your joy? Are you not in the hollow of my mantle, in the crossing of my arms? Do you need something more? Let nothing else worry you, disturb you …

—The Nican Mopohua, 118–119

God dwells on high, yet he stoops down to us … God is infinitely great, and far, far above us. This is our first experience of him. The distance seems infinite. The Creator of the universe, the one who guides all things, is very far from us: or so he seems at the beginning. But then comes the surprising realization: The One who has no equal, who "is seated on high", looks down upon us. He stoops down. He sees us, and he sees me. God's looking down is much more than simply seeing from above. God's looking is active. The fact that he sees me, that he looks at me, transforms me and the world around me … In looking down, he raises me up, he takes me gently by the hand and helps me—me!—to rise from depths towards the heights … That night in Bethlehem, it took on a completely new meaning … The Creator who holds all things in his hands, on whom we all depend, makes himself small and in need of human love.

— Christmas Homily, 25 December 2008
POPE BENEDICT XVI

NOTES

CONFERENCE
A Picture Worth a Thousand Words

INTRODUCTION

In the First Meditation, we prayerfully considered the actual events surrounding the apparitions of Our Lady of Guadalupe, and how they echoed the events surrounding Christ's birth. In the Second Meditation, we reflected prayerfully on some of the words that Our Lady spoke to St. Juan Diego throughout those wonderful, unforgettable days back in 1531. We saw how her words reiterated many of the most fundamental truths about our Christian faith. In this Conference, we will examine some characteristics of the miraculous image itself, and we will discover how they too reinforce the hopes and joys of the Advent and Christmas seasons.

A PRIVATE REVELATION

Before getting into the image, it is only fair to point out that plenty of critics have denied the authenticity of the events and the image of Our Lady of Guadalupe. These critics bring various arguments to bear in order to claim, basically, that the whole story was invented so as to trick the native Mexican people into becoming Christians.

Many Catholics have responded to those arguments and criticisms through in-depth research and investigation. And although some faith-motivated interpretations of the image do seem to make some exaggerated claims, the research in general is quite convincing in its support of authenticity.

The canonization of Juan Diego in 2002 and the insertion of the feast day of Our Lady of Guadalupe into the Church's liturgical calendar show that the official Catholic position is accepting of the authenticity, though the Church's main concern is the message contained in these events and image. Nevertheless, as with all approved Marian apparitions, the Church doesn't put its veracity on the level of dogma—Catholics are certainly not required to believe in Our Lady of Guadalupe, or Our Lady of Lourdes, or Our Lady of Fatima, with the same divine faith that we have regarding God's revelation in Christ of dogmas like the Incarnation, the Resurrection, and Jesus' Real Presence in the Eucharist.

Here is how the Catechism explains the value of approved private revelations like Our Lady of Guadalupe:

> Throughout the ages, there have been so-called "private" revelations, some of which have been recognized by the authority of the Church. They do not belong, however, to the deposit of faith. It is not their role to improve or complete Christ's definitive Revelation, but to help live mo re fully by it in a certain period of history. Guided by the Magisterium of the Church, the sensus fidelium [common sense of the faithful] knows how to discern and welcome in these revelations whatever constitutes an authentic call of Christ or his saints to the Church.

—CCC, 67

You can you can learn more about the various criticisms and investigations from the books listed in the "Further Reading" section at the end of this conference. For now, let's take a look at the most evident symbolism contained in this amazing image, and see how it continues to reflect and reinforce the Christmas message.

A COSMIC BACKGROUND

Let's begin with the background elements. We can see clearly that Mary is shown standing in front of the sun. The rays of the sun shine out from behind her, creating a kind of halo all around her. At the same time, she is shown standing on top of the moon, which is in a crescent phase. These two features immediately identify the figure with the woman referred to in the Book of Revelation:

> *A great sign appeared in the sky, a woman clothed with the sun, with the moon under her feet, and on her head a crown of twelve stars. She was with child and wailed aloud in pain as she labored to give birth.*
>
> —Revelation 12:1–2

Catholic liturgy and Catholic spiritual writers throughout history have seen in this biblical passage a reference to the Blessed Virgin Mary, as well as a reference to the Church itself, of which Mary has always been considered a theological type. From a biblical perspective, the sun, the moon, and the stars show the cosmic repercussions of the coming of Christ. In the eyes of the Mexican natives who first beheld Our Lady of Guadalupe, it would have meant something much more concrete.

They may not have been familiar with the biblical passage from the Book of Revelation, but they were very familiar with the sun and the moon. As a pre-industrial advanced civilization, their entire worldview was built around the seasons and rhythms of the agricultural year, which were measured through solar, and ritual calendars. As a pre-secularized pagan culture, their religious practices and beliefs were intricately intertwined with that same worldview. They recognized their dependence on the forces of nature, which were beyond their control, and so they attributed divine powers to the indicators of these forces—the sun and the moon. Some native beliefs saw the sun and the moon as being gods who were constantly in conflict, and religious sacrificial offerings were made to help sustain the sun in that cosmic battle.

In this context, the third element of the background, the angel beneath and supporting the moon, whose many-colored wings are shaped like the wings of an eagle, is also significant. The eagle was a sacred bird for the Aztec people, the leaders of the empire that ruled over Mexico at the time. It had a mythological role in Aztec origins, and an ongoing role in Aztec worship.

A NEW HARMONY

All these natural and symbolic elements are subordinated to and harmonized by the figure of Mary in the image of Our Lady of Guadalupe. For the native Mexicans, this would have spoken eloquently about the relationship between their ancient religious worldview and the new view being proposed by Christianity. The Christian worldview wasn't threatening to destroy the hopes of their ancient civilization, but rather it was bringing their hopes to fulfillment, and even surpassing them through a new, more complete revelation of divine truth. Here is how a native Mexican expressed this meaning during an interview in modern times:

> With the harmony of the angel, who holds up the Heavens and the Earth, a new life will come forth. This is what we received from our elders, our grandparents, that our lives do not end, but rather that they have a new meaning... This is

what we celebrate today [the feast of Our Lady of Guadalupe]… the arrival of this sign of unity, of harmony, of new life.[2]

But the eloquent symbolism doesn't end there. When we turn our attention to the figure of Mary herself, we can see how almost every detail is loaded with meaning from the native Mexican point of view.

CLOTHED WITH MEANING

First of all, the blue-green cloak decorated with stars would have reminded the Mexicans of the blue mantle decorated with emeralds, symbolizing the heavens, which was worn by the Aztec Emperor. The Virgin's tunic, on the other hand, more earthly in color and decorated with flowers, symbolized the earth. That the angel beneath her holds the ends of both garments shows that her authority and her message embrace the entire universe, the entire cosmos.

Next we turn to the dark ribbon tied above the Virgin's waist. We can see the ends of it hanging below her folded hands. This was a typical feature of women's clothing among the Mexicans, but it was usually worn lower, around the waist itself. It was only worn higher up, as in the case of the image, when a woman was pregnant. This clearly emphasizes Mary's role as mother, the Advent mother patiently awaiting the birth of Jesus.

---

2   Anderson and Chavez, p 36

A CODE IN FLOWERS

But who is her child? This too appears in the symbolism, through the flower outlined exactly underneath the ends of the dark ribbon, over Mary's womb. Three types of floral images decorate Mary's tunic: an isolated eight-petaled flower, which appears eight times (a symbol of birth and new life); a flower cluster including a curved stem and triangular blossom, which appears nine times; and a four-petaled jasmine flower, which appears only once. It is this flower that adorns the portion of Mary's tunic covering her womb, and its many-layered symbolism for the native peoples would have clearly indicated the uniquely divine nature of this woman's child.

It's interesting to note that all these floral designs are two-dimensional. They don't undulate with the folds and the shadows of Our Lady's clothing, which is depicted in three dimensions. This detail indicates that they are more than just decorations. They are actually reminiscent of a form of pictographic writing used by the Mexicans in that time period. These pictographs would be placed on square pages and be "read" from different angles. The flower cluster on Mary's tunic, for example, could symbolize "civilization", by its similarity to a hill near a river. But viewed from a different angle, it could also symbolize a heart with its artery connected to the Virgin's mantle—a clear reference to divine life coming to earth through Mary's mediation.

A MAJESTIC, HUMBLE QUEEN

The Jasmine flower isn't the only link to Jesus in the image. Around Mary's neck we also see a small brooch decorated with a black cross. Missionaries at the time preferred to use empty crosses when they spoke about Christ's passion and resurrection, because they thought that a crucifix might confusingly evoke memories of human sacrifices used in Aztec religion.

Above the brooch, Mary's face offers a tranquil and respectful countenance, emphasized by the tilt of her head and the averted glance of her eyes—both gestures indicating to the Mexicans that this celestial figure of Mary is offering a hospitable welcome to the viewer, while clearing not claiming to be divine herself.

This humility also appears in the position of her feet and of her hands. Mary's hands, for the Spaniards at the time and for the Mexicans who had already had contact with the missionaries, would have clearly indicated that she is at prayer. But in traditional native religious practices, prayer was not only expressed in words and song, but also in movement, in solemn dance. The image shows Mary engaging in this kind of prayer as well. She is shown lifting one knee in what would have clearly been interpreted as a dance step. Mary, manifested in the image as a heavenly queen through her imperial garb and cosmic symbols, is also shown as the humble handmaid whose queenship clearly flows from her beautiful worship of and submission to God.

Finally, the color of her skin is also remarkable. Mary shows herself to be what is called *mestiza*. That is, her skin is a mixed color: not so light as the typical Spaniard, and not so dark as the typical Mexican, she shares the characteristics of both ethnic groups. Here again, we see Mary building a bridge between cultures, harmonizing in her image the differences that were threatening to tear apart this society in the aftermath of the Europeans' arrival to the New World.

Through all these visual elements, Our Lady of Guadalupe is helping to translate Christ and the Christian message into a language that could be understood and savored by the native Mexicans. The miraculous image's attention to so many details makes its appearance very similar to the appearance of Christ at the first Christmas, when God unmistakably revealed his care and his interest in each of us, simply by becoming one of us.

Take some time now to reflect prayerfully on the personal questionnaire in the Companion Guide, which is designed to help you draw some personal applications from this historical and spiritual reflection.

PERSONAL QUESTIONNAIRE

1. Which symbols from the image of Our Lady of Guadalupe strike me most deeply? Why? How is the Lord hoping that I will respond to them?

2. How is God reaching out to me personally—in the events and contexts unique to my life—this Advent? How am I responding?

3. One of Mary's titles in Catholic spirituality is "Queen of Apostles." In my own words, how does the apparition of Our Lady of Guadalupe show that Mary is a model Christian apostle/missionary?

4. How am I being a Christian apostle/missionary in my own family? What lessons from Our Lady of Guadalupe can help me be a better one?

5. How am I being a Christian apostle/missionary in my work/community? What lessons from Our Lady of Guadalupe can help me be a better one?

6. How am I being a Christian apostle/missionary in my society/culture? What lessons from Our Lady of Guadalupe can help me be a better one?

7. The Church's liturgical calendar—including seasons like Advent and feasts like Our Lady of Guadalupe and Christmas—is meant to help all Catholics live their faith deeply and experience the joy of God's love in the midst of their daily lives. How much am I benefiting from this gift (the liturgical calendar) that God wants to give me?

8. What can I do so that my life is more in harmony with the rhythms of the liturgy?

9. What can I do to help my family life be more in harmony with the rhythms of the liturgy?

NOTES

FURTHER READING

If you feel moved to continue reflecting and praying about this theme, you may find the following books helpful:

Our Lady of Guadalupe: Mother of the Civilization of Love,
by Carl Anderson and Msgr. Eduardo Chávez

The Wonder of Guadalupe
by Francis Johnston

"Apparitions and Private Revelations"
Colin B Donavan, STL
https://www.ewtn.com/expert/answers/apparitions.htm
(referenced 9 March 2018)

EXPLORING MORE

Please visit our website, *RCSpirituality.org,* for more spiritual resources, and follow us on Facebook for regular updates: *facebook.com/RCSpirituality.*

If you would like to support and sponsor a Retreat Guide, please consider making a donation at RCSpirituality.org.

Retreat Guides are a service of Regnum Christi.
RegnumChristi.org

Produced by Coronation Media.
CoronationMedia.com

Developed & Self-published by RCSpirituality.
RCSpirituality.org

Made in the USA
Coppell, TX
26 September 2023

22055254R00036